Coffee Talk

A Celebration of
Good Coffee and Great Friends

Ellyn Sanna

HUMBLECREEK
INSPIRATION FOR LIFE

© 1999 by Barbour Publishing, Inc.

ISBN 1-59310-394-8

Scripture quotations marked NLT are taken from the *Holy Bible*, New Living Translation, copyright ©1996. Used by permission of Tyndale House Publishers, Inc., Wheaton, Illinois 60189, U.S.A. All rights reserved.

Scripture quotations marked NIV are taken from the HOLY BIBLE: NEW INTERNATIONAL VERSION®. NIV®. Copyright © 1973, 1978, 1984 by International Bible Society. Used by permission of Zondervan Publishing House. All rights reserved.

Published by Humble Creek, P.O. Box 719, Uhrichsville, Ohio 44683

Printed in China.
5 4 3 2 1

Contents

Our world loves coffee. People find drinking a cup of coffee to be a private ritual, a peaceful little space of time that gives their day structure and significance. Even more, coffee is a social ceremony, something we do while we talk with friends. It provides us with moments of relaxation in the midst of our workday.

With caffeine or without, coffee is more than a simple beverage. The very aroma of fresh-ground coffee beans carries with it a whole bundle of feel-good sensations: warmth, comfort, friendship, relaxation, hospitality, intimacy.

A Ceremony of Friendship

Every true friend is a glimpse of God.

LUCY LARCOM

When friends meet, hearts warm.

PROVERB

"Come over for a cup of coffee," we say to our friends. What we really mean is, "Let's spend some time together talking." An invitation for coffee is synonymous with an offer of friendship; it means we want to take the time to get to know each other better. In our culture, drinking coffee together has somehow become one of friendship's building blocks, a small and casual ceremony that brings us closer to each other.

*Holy Friendship that has medicine for
all the wretchedness is not to be despised.
From God it truly is, that amid the wretchedness of this exile,
we be comforted with the counsel of friends
until we come to Him.*

RICHARD ROLLE (1300–1349)

A friend is a present you give yourself.

ROBERT LOUIS STEVENSON

*Do you know that conversation is one of
the greatest pleasures in life?*

SOMERSET MAUGHAM

A person standing alone can be attacked and defeated,
but two can stand back-to-back and conquer.
Three are even better, for a triple-braided cord
is not easily broken.

ECCLESIASTES 4:12 NLT

How it dissolves the barriers that divide us, and loosens all constraint,
and diffuses itself like some fine old cordial through
all the veins of life—this feeling that we understand
and trust each other,
and wish each other heartily well!

HENRY VAN DYKE

The greatest gift we can give one another is
rapt attention to one another's existence.

SUE ATCHLEY EBAUGH

What a thing friendship is, world without end!
How it gives the heart and soul a stir-up!

ROBERT BROWNING

True friends don't spend time gazing into each other's eyes.
They may show great tenderness toward each other,
but they face in the same direction—toward common projects,
interests, goals—above all, toward a common Lord.

C. S. LEWIS

Friendship renders prosperity more brilliant,
while it lightens adversity by sharing it
and making its burden common.

CICERO

If you want to improve your understanding, drink coffee.

SYDNEY SMITH

One of the most beautiful qualities of true friendship is
to understand and to be understood.

SENECA

To have joy one must share it—
Happiness was born a twin.

LORD BYRON

I find friendship to be. . .
the true. . .
restorative cordial.

THOMAS JEFFERSON

Friendships multiply joys and divide griefs.

H. G. BOHN

A Private Ritual

Go on loving what is good, simple, and ordinary.
RAINER MARIA RILKE

Coffee is the common man's gold, and like gold,
it brings to every man the feeling of luxury and nobility.
ABD-AL-KADIR, 1587

Coffee played a big role in our life.
The first thing you did in the morning was put on water,
and the last thing you did at night was take off the pot.

PAUL PRUDHOMME, quoted by John DeMers,

The Community Kitchen's Complete Guide to Gourmet Coffee

As human beings, we need to impose some sort of structure onto the great chaotic mass of life. Otherwise, we too easily lose our way amid the welter of emotions and events. We use weddings and graduations and funerals for some of the biggest of life's events—but we also have small, private ceremonies that are useful for the ordinary, everyday business. We tend to take these little daily rituals for granted, but our life would be the poorer without them, for these are the moments when we can touch God.

What are these personal ceremonies? I'm sure they're different for each of us. But for me, that morning cup of coffee is somehow essential to the day's progress. Almost mindlessly, I grind the beans, smelling their aroma, and put them in the filter. Then I wait while the coffee maker sighs and drips, and the odor fills the kitchen. At last, I sit down at the table, my cup in hand, looking out at the dogwood tree while I slowly sip the coffee and open my heart to God. By the time I'm done, the kids are pounding down the stairs, and it's time to make breakfast and lunches, braid hair and find matching socks, make sure faces are washed and teeth brushed. But that's okay, because I'm ready now.

That cup of coffee is just a small moment in my life, a quiet little space that somehow opens the day's door, so that I can walk through with a calmer spirit, out into my life's activity.

Sweetening one's coffee is generally
the first stirring event of the day.

ANONYMOUS

When you pray, go away by yourself. . .
and pray to your Father secretly. Then your Father,
who knows all secrets, will reward you.

MATTHEW 6:6 NLT

Teach us delight in simple things.

RUDYARD KIPLING

I have measured out my life with coffee spoons.
T. S. ELIOT, *The Love Song of J. Alfred Prufrock*

Coffee Breaks: Tiny Sabbaths

The Sabbath is a sign of the covenant between me and you forever.
It helps you to remember that I am the LORD, who makes you holy.
Work six days only, but the seventh day must be a day of total rest.

EXODUS 31:13, 15 NLT

Where our work is, there let our joy be.

TERTULLIAN, C. 220

The Hebrew word *sabbath* means simply "rest." When God made us, He knew we would need to rest from our work; and apparently He also knew how hard that would be for some of us, for He made the sabbath not merely a suggestion, but a commandment. Sabbath times are not to be refused because we're too busy; instead, we should "make every effort to enter that rest" (Heb. 4:11 NIV). These are times when we separate ourselves from the business of life so that we can be refreshed and renewed.

For many of us, we find a little sabbath in the midst of each workday: our coffee break. This is the moment in our busy schedule when we can pause and relax. Over a hot cup of coffee, we laugh with friends and momentarily draw away from the day's pressures. Or we sit alone at our desk, drinking in peace and a renewed sense of perspective alone with our coffee.

Either way, this is a moment we can offer to God. Historically, God's people have connected sabbath times with worship, for when we take time from our work, we clear our minds so that we can think consciously about God.

Research shows that people work quicker and more efficiently if they're give regular coffee breaks. Savor the full gift of these small sabbaths.

Coffee detracts nothing from your intellect; on the contrary,
your stomach is freed by it and no longer distresses your brain;
it will not hamper your mind with troubles
but give freedom to its working.
Suave molecules of Mocha stir up your blood, without causing excessive heat; the organ of thought receives from it a feeling of sympathy; work becomes easier and you sit down without distress.

PRINCE TALLEYRAND (1754–1838)

The Aroma of Love

If I were a woman, I'd wear coffee as a perfume.
JOHN VAN DRUTEN

Where coffee is served there is grace and splendor.
ANONYMOUS

To a coffee lover, nothing smells so good as fresh coffee beans. My sister has a friend who loves the aroma so much that each time she opens a new can of coffee, she holds it out to her children and commands them to breathe deeply. "Whenever you smell this in life," she says, "think of me." She can think of no better thing to which to tie her memory, and she hopes that when her children are old and she is long dead, that rich, dark smell will speak to them of the same love and acceptance that she offered them.

Keep on loving each other. . . .
Do not forget to entertain strangers,
for by so doing some people have
entertained angels without knowing it.

HEBREWS 13:1–2 NIV

The first time I drank coffee was when I was in high school. The guidance counselor and his secretary kept a pot hot for any students who wandered into their office. I remember how welcoming the smell was, how much it spoke to me of maturity and comfort. High school wasn't always a very easy world; I didn't quite fit the mold that would have made me accepted and popular, and adolescent anguish is particularly painful. But in the guidance office, breathing that warm, dark brown aroma while I sipped the grown-up brew, I caught a glimpse of a world where I'd fit, a world of ideas and words and laughter.

You are as welcome as flowers in May.

WILLIAM SHAKESPEARE

I had a perfect honeymoon. Sometimes reality falls short of our fantasies, but not this time. We walked the cobblestone streets of Quebec City hand in hand, poking our heads into quaint little shops, eating in cozy, European restaurants while we looked into each other's eyes. My husband practiced his French while we bought each other gifts—a leather briefcase I still carry, a carved head of a proud African woman that stands on our bookcase now. And every morning we'd drink *café au lait,* strong and sweet, with our croissants.

Fourteen years and three kids later, my husband and I don't have much time in our day for looking into each other's eyes. Mornings, I'm already at my desk working while he hurries to get dressed and out the door. We pass each other in the kitchen usually, where we grab a quick kiss while I make us each a cup of *café au lait.*

But to my mind, the coffee's even stronger and sweeter than it was in Quebec City.

> *Good coffee is black as sin,*
> *pure as the angels,*
> *strong as death,*
> *and sweet as love.*
>
> Creole saying

A History of Hospitality, Good Conversation, and Prayer

Share with God's people. . . .
Practice hospitality.

ROMANS 12:13 NIV

With modern society in the throes of a love affair with coffee, historians have tried to tie coffee to the writings of the ancient world. After all, how could ancient people have survived without coffee? The very idea is hard to imagine.

That's why some have claimed that Homer mentions coffee; they insist that the *nepenthe* that Helen of Troy brought with her from Egypt, sort of her hostess gift, must have actually been our favorite brew. Others say that the Lacedaemonians' "black broth," a part of their traditional hospitality, was obviously coffee. And then of course, we'd all like to find coffee in the Bible; surely David must have written a psalm about it *somewhere.* Or what about the red pottage for which Esau sold his birthright? Who would do that for a bowl of lentils, after all? But for a cup of coffee? Well, that we can understand. Or how about the parched grain that Boaz ordered for Ruth? Makes sense, doesn't it, that he was doing what we all do when we're feeling hospitable—offering his guest a nice hot cup of coffee? And remember when Abigail gave David five measures of parched corn, hoping to appease his wrath? Well, obviously the translators used the word *corn* loosely, because what the original author must have meant is probably five hospitable canisters of roasted coffee beans. Right?

Actually, however, coffee originated in the Arab world. One legend says that a goat herder named Kaldi, who lived in upper Egypt or Abyssinia, noticed that his goats were more lively after crunching on a particular kind of cherry. After watching his goats "abandoning themselves to the most extravagant prancing," Kaldi decided he might as well try the fruit himself. Soon after, a monk from the nearby monastery was surprised to see Kaldi and his goats leaping and prancing with unusual energy. The monks experimented with boiling the cherries—and to their surprise, they found that the dark drink helped them pray better. Instead of falling asleep over their evening devotions, they came to God with refreshed alertness. Coffee had been discovered.

The Turks have a drink of black colour. . . .
They swallow it hot as it comes from the fire
and they drink it in long draughts, not at dinner time,
but as a kind of dainty and sipped slowly
while talking with one's friends.
One cannot find any meetings among them
where they drink it not. . . .

ITALIAN EXPLORER, 1615

The Arabs and Egyptians make a sort of decoction of it,
which they drink instead of wine:
and it is sold in all their public houses. . . .

PROSPERO ALPINI, 1580

As European explorers ventured into the Arab world in the sixteenth century, they encountered coffee for the first time. They were so taken with the new beverage that they were certain it must have medicinal properties. By the seventeenth century, they had brought it with them back to their own countries and coffee houses spread throughout Europe. As European countries colonized the West Indies and South America, they discovered that coffee could be grown there quite profitably.

Closes the Orifice of the Stomack, fortifies the Heat within, helpeth Digestion, quickneth the Spirits, makes the Heart lightsom, is good against Eye-sores, Coughs, or Colds, Rhumes, Consumptions, Head-ach, Dropsie, Gout, Scurvy. . . and many others.

PUBLICK ADVISER, 1657

This Rare Arabian cordial Use, then thou may'st all the Doctors' shops refuse.

ADVERTISEMENT FROM 1674

Choicest Mocha coffee [served] *in*
tiny cups of egg-shell porcelain,
hot, strong, and fragrant,
poured out in saucers of gold and silver. . .
to the grand dames, who fluttered their fans
with many grimaces, bending their piquant faces. . .
over the new and steaming beverage.

Isaac D'Israeli, *Curiosities of Literature*

During the Enlightenment, coffee houses became the spiritual and intellectual centers for new thoughts about democracy and human equality. These coffee houses became known as penny universities, for anyone craving intellectual stimulation could pay for it with the cost of a cup of coffee—one penny.

In the New World, Daniel Webster called a Boston coffee house, the Green Dragon, the "headquarters of the Revolution." Early English settlers may have preferred tea, but with one fell swoop, the Boston Tea Party in 1773 created a country of coffee drinkers.

Hot, black and
strong enough to walk by itself.
19th-century coffee preference,
JOEL, DAVID, & KARL SCHAPIRA,
The Book of Coffee and Tea

Mass consumption of coffee began in the 1800s. The stimulating beverage had found itself a permanent home in the workplaces created by the Industrial Revolution. It helped workers get through their grueling sixteen-hour workdays, and it kept them awake long enough at home to interact with their families. Coffee was a fixture in most everyone's life.

Today, coffee grows throughout the world in tropical and subtropical regions. The trees require a constant temperature and sixty to eighty inches of annual rain.

Coffee plants are actually an evergreen shrub. They produce jasmine-scented white blossoms that mature into red cherries. The coffee bean is the fruit's seed; two beans grow face-to-face within each cherry. Each tree produces only a pound to a pound and a half of roasted coffee each year—about four thousand hand-picked beans.

Arabica and robusta are the two different species of coffee trees. Arabica grows in the mountains, and it is the coffee used for today's popular specialty coffees. Robusta grows at lower altitudes. It has twice the caffeine content as arabica, and it is used for instant and commercial coffees.

CAFFEINE OR DECAF?

Caffeine is a mild stimulant that's found in coffee, tea, chocolate, cola, and headache medicine. Tolerance to caffeine varies from person to person, but for most of us, caffeine acts merely as a gentle aid to thought, productivity, and conversation.

Decaffeinated coffee is created by removing the caffeine from the green coffee beans. One method uses a solvent to pull the caffeine out of the beans while leaving the flavors intact. The solvent vaporizes when the beans are then roasted. Another method, the Swiss Water Process, submerges the beans in very hot water and then percolates the water through activated charcoal. The beans are then returned to the water to reabsorb the flavorful oils. This method is slightly more expensive.

Coffee Roast

LIGHT ROAST:

cinnamon-colored, sour tasting. Most commercial canned coffee is light roasted.

MEDIUM ROAST:

chestnut-colored, full range of flavors. Used for specialty coffees.

DARK ROAST:

the color of bittersweet chocolate, oily, with a smoky and bitter taste. Used for Espresso and Italian coffees.

VERY DARK ROAST:

black, oily, bitter. Used in French coffees.

Recipes

Old-Fashioned Coffee Soda

3 cups chilled double-strength
   soda
1 tablespoon sugar
1 cup half-and-half

4 scoops (1 pint) coffee
   ice cream
¾ cup chilled club soda
whipped cream for garnish

Combine the coffee and sugar. Blend in the half-and-half. Fill four tall glasses halfway with the coffee mixture. Add a scoop of ice cream to each glass. Fill to the top with soda. Add a dollop of whipped cream to each glass.

COFFEE TIP

Too fine a grind causes a bitter brew, because the beans have more surface area where they can be exposed to the water. Too coarse a grind results in watery coffee, because the water runs through the coffee too quickly.

Coffee Pecan Pie

COMBINE:

3 eggs

¼ cup molasses

½ cup double strength coffee

¼ tsp salt

¾ cup light corn syrup

2 tbsps melted butter

1 tsp vanilla

ADD:

1 cup chopped pecans

4 tbsps flour

Pour ingredients into an unbaked pie shell. Bake 40 to 45 minutes at 375 degrees, or until firm. Garnish with whipped cream.

Coffee is the crowning of a grand dinner. . .
the piéce de rèsistance. . . .

LAFCADIO HEARN, *La Cuisine Creolee,*

19th-century cookbook

Coffee Cake

2 cups flour

½ tsp baking soda

¼ tsp allspice

¼ tsp nutmeg

½ cup chopped walnuts or pecans

¼ cup brown sugar

3 eggs

1 tsp baking powder

dash of salt

¼ tsp ground cloves

¼ tsp ginger

½ cup butter

½ cup honey

½ cup coffee

Bake in a 9-inch square pan at 350 degrees for 35-45 minutes. Dust with confectioners' sugar.

COFFEE TIP

Air and moisture quickly steal coffee's flavorful oils. To keep the coffee's flavor, buy and store whole beans; grind them only when you're ready to use them immediately. Store beans in an airtight container in the freezer.

Chocolate Swirl Coffee Cake

STIR TOGETHER:
⅓ cup flaked coconut
¼ cup sugar

⅓ cup chopped nuts
1 tbsp melted butter or
   margarine

Set aside.

MIX:
2 cups Bisquick
1 egg
2 tbsps melted butter or margarine

¼ cup sugar
¾ cup milk

Pour into 8x8-inch square pan. Spoon ⅓ cup melted chocolate chips over batter and cut with a knife several times to make a marbled effect. Sprinkle coconut mixture evenly over the top. Bake 20 to 25 minutes in a 400-degree oven.

Eat, O friends, and drink;
drink your fill.

SONG OF SOLOMON 5:1 NIV

For the happy heart,
life is a continual feast.

PROVERBS 15:15 NLT

Enjoy!